Based on NCS

Four Seasons English

Listening & Speaking, Reading & Writing

정은주(Eun Joo Jeong)
고인숙(Inn Sook Koh)
심재황(Jaehwang Shim)

CD포함

양성원

머리말

그 동안 여러 차례 교육과정을 통하여 사회에서 요구하는 영어교육이 이루어지고 있습니다. 특히 제7차 교육과정(2000-2008) 이후 의사소통 능력 (Communicative Competence)과 더불어, 음성교육(Listening and Speaking)의 비중이 더욱 강화되었습니다. 영어 학습 교재에 있어서, 다양한 과제 활동(task activity)을 위한 많은 자료가 개발되고 있지만 이러한 교재들은 대부분 학생들의 흥미와 이해에 중점을 둔 과제 활동에 관한 내용들로 구성되어 있습니다.

최근 대학교에서는 학생들에게 직업 업무를 수행할 수 있는 실제 영어활용 능력을 요구하고 있습니다. 또한 입사지원자들은 실제 직업에 대한 업무수행 능력을 측정할 수 있도록 고안된 새로운 고용 틀인 **국가직무능력표준(National Competency Standards : NCS)**에 맞추어야 합니다. 따라서 영어를 학습하는 대학생들은 이 직무능력에 적합한 학습 교재와 학습 방법을 준비하여 공기업체와 일반 회사의 취업을 위해 준비해야 합니다.

이 교재는 현재 영어 교육과정의 내용과 지침에 맞도록 학습자의 흥미에 중점을 두었으며, 사회에서 요구하는 직무능력시험에 내비하도록 구성되었습니다. 또한 학습자들이 다양한 상황에 주어진 학습 내용을 통하여 영어의 의사소통 능력을 키우고, 그 능력이 자신이 원하는 업무에서 실제로 활용이 가능하도록 구성하였습니다.

단원 마다 주요 필수 표현(Key Expressions)에 바탕을 두고, 듣기 능력(Listening Skill), 말하기 능력(Speaking Skill), 읽기 능력(Reading Skill) 그리고 쓰기 능력(Writing Skill)을 단계별로 구성하였습니다. 이 교재에 제시된 다양한 과제활동의 이해와 연습을 통하여 자연스런 **영어 의사소통능력**에 도달하는 것을 목표로 하며, 졸업 후 직장에서 요구하는 **영어 직무능력 향상**에 도움이 되기를 기대합니다.

2017년 1월
저자 드림

Contents

Listening Skill (의사 청취 능력)

Contents

Part Ⅱ

Speaking Skill (의사 표현 능력)

Contents

Reading Skill (문서 이해 능력)

Part Ⅳ

Writing Skill (문서 작성 능력)

Memo

Part I

Listening Skill

(의사 청취 능력)

Unit 1. Restaurant and Food

Unit 2. Emotion and Feeling

Unit 3. Fashion and Hobby

Unit 4. Friendship and Personal Problem

Unit 5. Health and Care

Unit 6. Housing and Facilities

Unit

1. Restaurant and Food

Expressions at a restaurant ordering food and payment

Key Expressions

1. Are you ready to order now?
2. I'll have some salad, roast beef, and potatoes.
3. How do you want your beef?
4. Rare, medium, or well-done.
5. Which one would you like, coffee or tea?
6. Half sliced and the other half diced.
7. I'm going to cook some chicken.
8. Are you sure the meat is fresh?
9. Don't tell me. You already ate them all.
10. Let's eat out this dinner, shall we?
11. Can you sometimes cook for yourself?
12. What would you recommend?

Dialogue 1. Do you have coffee or tea?

Waitress : Are you ready to order now?

Adam : Yes. I'll have some salad, roast beef, and potatoes.

Waitress : How do you want your beef?
Rare, medium, or well-done?

Adam : Well-done, please.

Waitress : Sure. Anything to drink?

Adam : Do you have coffee or tea? I'd like something hot.

Waitress : Yes, we have both.
Which one would you like, coffee or tea?

Adam : Hot tea, please. And with some milk.

Dialogue 2. Can you help me cut this chicken?

Lillian : John, can you do me a favor?
Can you help me cut this chicken?

John : Sure. No problem. How do you want me to cut it?

Lillian : I would like half of it cut into slices.
And the other half diced.

John : OK. Half sliced and the other half diced.

Lillian : Oh, by the way, I want it to be very lean.
Can you do it for me?

John : Yes, you want to cut off the fat.
You mean you don't like the fat on the meat.

Dialogue 3. Why don't we eat out?

George : What are you going to eat for dinner?

Grace : I'm going to cook some chicken.

George : Are you sure the meat is fresh?

Grace : Yes, I bought it the day before yesterday.

George : But you forgot to put it in the refrigerator.

Grace : Oh, that's too bad. Now what should we do?

George : Why don't we eat out?

Grace : Again? Where are we going?
Let's find the restaurant that is not expensive.

George : Yes, we are hungry.

Dialogue 4. I like cookies flavored with chocolate.

Mary : John, where are the cookies and salad?

John : Don't tell me. You already ate them all.

Mary : Yes, I did. But I couldn't help it.
The taste was so good.

John : I thought you didn't like salad.

Mary : Well, I don't like salad.
But I like cookies flavored with chocolate.
I love them to death.

John : Umm, I didn't know that.

Mary : Chocolate cookies taste better than anything.

Dialogue 5. What about Chinese restaurant?

Jimmy : Let's eat out for dinner, shall we?

Dolly : I'd like to but sorry. I'm broke recently.
I've got through my paycheck for the week.

Jimmy : Don't worry about it. It's my treat.
I can pay for dinner. Just follow me.

Dolly : Are you sure? You're so generous.

Jimmy : Don't say like that. We are good friends, you know?

Dolly : So, where are you taking me?

Jimmy : What about the Chinese restaurant?

Dolly : That's quite a good place. Let's go there.

Dialogue 6. How often do you eat out?

Paul : How often do you eat out, Stella?

Stella : Well, I eat out almost three or four times a week.
Do you think it is very often?

Paul : Wow, I really envy you.
You often enjoy some delicious tastes.

Stella : Don't envy me. It's for business.
In fact, I'm sick and tired of restaurant food.
I want a home-cooked meal.

Paul : Can you sometimes cook for yourself?
What would you recommend?

Stella : No. Don't say that. I am poor at cooking food.

Review Exercise

Write the answer to the question in English and the meaning in Korean.

1. How do you want your beef? Rare, medium, or well-done?

____.

2. Do you have coffee or tea? I'd like something hot.

____.

3. Can you help me cut this chicken?

____.

4. How do you want me to cut it?

____.

5. What are you going to eat for dinner?

____.

6. Are you sure the meat is fresh?

____.

7. Now what should we do?

____.

8. Where are we going?

____.

9. Why don't we eat out?

____.

10. Where are we going?

____.

Unit

2. Emotion and Feeling

The expressions of good memory, past experience, or personality

Key Expressions

1. Can you do the dishes for me tonight?
2. I've also had a very hard day.
3. Why are you being such a selfish man?
4. I will try to be better next time.
5. Is there something bad in particular?
6. Take it easy. You are so angry, aren't you?
7. You look concerned. What's the matter with you?
8. I should finish a report this week.
9. What's going on between you and Alex?
10. What do you think of him?
11. I told him that he could be more patient.
12. I will not give him an advice any more.

Dialogue 1. Just leave me alone today.

Anne : Jack, can you do the dishes for me tonight?
I'm very tired.

Jack : I've also had a very hard day.
I want to kick back and relax from now.

Anne : Hey! Just because you had a bad day.
You are so selfish, aren't you?

Jack : I'm sorry. Just leave me alone today.

Anne : Why are you being such a selfish man?
I wish I hadn't got married.

Jack : Please leave me alone today.
I will try to be better next time.

Dialogue 2. He turned me down.

Grace : What happened now, Alex?
You weren't very kind when you were talking with your friend.

Alex : I don't like him any more.

Grace : Why? Is there anything bad in particular?

Alex : Well, he is such a mean guy.
I went to his office to ask him for some help.
And he turned me down.
I was so angry.
He wasn't like that before.

Grace : Take it easy. You are so angry, aren't you?
Do you want my advice?

Alex : Of course, I know you're right.

Grace : I will call and tell him not to turn down.

Alex : Thanks. I hope he will be my friend again.

Dialogue 3. Don't worry about it too much.

Jason : Hey, you look concerned. What's the matter with you?

Marry : I have a big problem. The final exam.
I'm not prepared for it yet. It's not easy.

Jason : Well, don't worry about it too much.
You still have three days. That's enough time.

Marry : Yeah, but I have another one.
I should finish a report this week.
Three days is not enough for me.

Jason : I will give you some copies that summarize the key points.
They will be helpful for your exam.

Marry : Thank you so much. You are so kind.

Jason : You're welcome. Then when do you need them?

Marry : As soon as possible. I need them right now.

Dialogue 4. I have tried to be good with him.

Sophia : What's going on between you and Alex?

Andy : I have tried to be good with him.
But I can't stand him any more.

Sophia : What do you think of him?

Andy : He is so short minded, I think.
So, he doesn't accept my friendly advice.

Sophia : So what did you tell him?

Andy : I told him that he could be more patient.
I hope he tries not to lose his temper so easily.

Sophia : I see. He should be more patient for friends.

Andy : I will not give him an advice any more.

Sophia : No. You can try to help your friend. I will help you, too.

Dialogue 5. I think you need to take it easy.

Mary : You look so angry. What happened?

Alex : Nothing. I'd rather not talk about it.
Don't ask me anything.

Mary : Come on. I think you need to take it easy.
You shouldn't keep your feelings with you.
They'll hurt your health. So, talk to me.

Alex : All right. This morning I took my car to the garage.
I wanted to have them check the engine.
But the car had a noise again.

Mary : Sorry to hear that. I'd be mad, too.

Alex : Yeah. And they were rude.
They didn't explain the condition in detail.

Mary : You should complain about it.

Dialogue 6. You look so worried.

Sara : You look so tired. What's the matter?

Jimmy : I didn't sleep well last night.

Sara : Did you have something on your mind?
You look so worried.

Jimmy : Yes, I have a big problem recently.

Sara : That's too bad. Maybe I can help you.

Jimmy : Well, I'm under a lot of pressure.
I have a presentation for the class next week.

Sara : Is there anything I can do to help you?

Jimmy : Well, I guess no one can help me.
I will try to do it for myself.

Sara : But I can do something for you.

Jimmy : Thanks. You're so kind.

Review Exercise

Write the answer to the question in English and the meaning in Korean.

1. Can you do the dishes for me tonight? I'm very tired.

____.

2. You are so selfish, aren't you?

____.

3. Why are you being such a selfish man?

____.

4. What happened now?

____.

5. Is there Anything bad in particular?

____.

6. You are so angry, aren't you? Do you want my advice?

____ .

7. You look concerned. What's the matter with you?

____ .

8. Then when do you need them?

____ .

9. What’s going on?

____ .

10. What do you think of him?

____ .

Unit

3. Fashion and Hobby

Favorite things to do and various hobbies to enjoy

Key Expressions

1. Look at this catalog of the shopping mall.
2. What's on your mind? You have one already.
3. This was last year's style.
4. I can't understand the trend. It's waste of money.
5. I'm sure that I still look pretty.
6. I heard it may soften the skin.
7. I don't know what's happening.
8. Come on. Stop joking.
9. I am worried. And what shall I do to stop it?
10. Her hair style looks funny, doesn't it?
11. That style went out last year.
12. You know I'm a little out of style.

Dialogue 1. This was last year's style.

Candy : Look at this catalog of the shopping mall.
They have a special sale.
Swimming suit is on sale.

John : What's on your mind? You have one already.

Candy : But I bought it a long time ago.

John : Yes. but it is just one year.
Don't you think one year is long?

Candy : That's true. However, you don't understand.
This was last year's style.

John : I think it looks perfect.
It hasn't gone out this year.

Candy : That's because you're not a woman.
Every summer, everybody wears new style.

John : I can't understand the trend. It's waste of money.

Dialogue 2. It may soften the skin.

Jason : She's really pretty. She looks so cute, doesn't she?

Beth : Well, I think that she puts lots of make-up on her face.

Jason : Umm... You are a little jealous of her appearance.

Beth : No. I don't have to put a lot of things on my face.
I'm sure that I still look pretty.
Don't you think so?

Jason : You're right. But can you recommend something for me to put on my face?

Beth : Let see. Cucumber is fine.
It's a natural skin soother. Natural healer of the skin.

Jason : It may soften the skin. Right?

Beth : Yes. It wipes out tight and tired feelings.
It also removes lines and age signs.

Jason : That's right. It is very useful, isn't it?

Dialogue 3. It really fixes skin in trouble.

Phil : I am serious. My foot feels very itchy.
I don't know what's happening.

Connie : Let me take a look. I think you have athlete's foot.

Phil : What are you talking about? I'm not an athlete.

Connie : Come on. Stop joking.
You'd better take care of it before it gets worse.

Phil : I am worried. And what shall I do to stop it?

Connie : I guess I've got some cream for it.
It really fixes skin in trouble.

Phil : Oh, thank you. Have you had athlete's foot before?

Connie : Yeah. It was a very bad experience.
You should keep your feet dry and clean.

Phil : Yes, I will do that. Can I get it now?

Connie : Here it is. Now apply it to the affected areas.

Dialogue 4. I'm a little out of style.

Cathy : Her hair style looks funny, doesn't it?

Daniel : I don't think so. I wouldn't say that.
It looks fine.

Cathy : She's behind the times.
That style went out last year.

Daniel : Come on. However, it looks good on her.

Cathy : Wow, you're really as out-dated as she is.

Daniel : You're right. You know I'm a little out of style.
What's the point of keeping yourself in style?

Cathy : I usually change my hair and dress.
So can you buy me some new dresses?

Daniel : Oh, I see. That's your point.

Dialogue 5. I will change my style.

Tom : Your dress looks funny.

Sara : I don’t think so. It looks fine to me.

Tom : Are you kidding? You are behind the times.
That style went out last year.

Sara : Oh, come on. I think it looks good on me.

Tom : Wow, you're really out-dated.

Sara : Well, you're right. I'm out of style.
I will change my style.

Tom : Good. If you change your dress, it will look good on you.

Sara : Thanks for your suggestion.

Dialogue 6. What kind of music do you like?

Andy : What kind of music do you like?

Beth : I like classical music most. Why?

Andy : I have tickets to a concert.
Do you want to go with me?

Beth : What music is it?

Andy : The Korean Symphony. They play Beethoven and Bruckner.

Beth : When is it?

Andy : At 8:00 PM. this Friday night.

Beth : Good. I'd like to go with you.
Where shall we meet?

Andy : We can meet at the subway station near the Art Center.

Beth : When shall we meet?

Andy : Let's meet at 6:00.
And we will have dinner first. Right?

Beth : Good idea. Thanks.

Review Exercise

Write the answer to the question in English and the meaning in Korean.

1. What's on your mind? You have one already.

____.

2. Don't you think one year is long?

____.

3. She's really pretty. She looks so cute, doesn't she?

____.

4. You are a little jealous of her appearance, aren't you?

____.

5. Can you recommend me to put on my face?

____.

6. What are you talking about? I'm not an athlete.

____ .

7. I am worried. And what shall I do to stop it?

____ .

8. Have you had athlete's foot before?

____ .

9. Yes, I will do that. Can I get it now?

____ .

10. Her hair style looks funny, doesn't it?

____ .

Unit 4. Friendship and Personal Problem

Meeting people and facing personal problems

Key Expressions

1. How is your new roommate?
2. What happened?
3. I have tried many times, but it didn't work.
4. I guess I'm going to complain to the manager.
5. You are going to move to L.A.
6. I'm going to miss you so much.
7. Let's keep in touch.
8. I will send my messages on e-mail, too.
9. I haven't seen you for a while.
10. There are plenty of fish in the sea.
11. You should be open-minded.
12. What are you going to do after you graduate?

Dialogue 1. I hope I will change my room again.

Alex : I heard you changed room at the dormitory.
How is your new roommate?

Margaret : I don't want to think of the friend.
She really turns me off.

Alex : What happened?

Margaret : She sometimes made loud noises at midnight.
And she seemed rude to me.

Alex : Why don't you have a heart to heart chat with her?

Margaret : I have tried many times, but it didn't work.
She made me upset.

Alex : How many times did you try?

Margaret : At least three or four times.
I'm going to complain to the manager.
I hope I will change my room again.

Dialogue 2. Do you have my e-mail address?

Anne : I heard you are going to move to LA.

Jimmy : Yes. I got an offer of another position from the LA office.

Anne : That's great. I will miss you so much.

Jimmy : Me too. Let's keep in touch.

Anne : Yeah. Don't forget to call me.

Jimmy : Sure. I will send my messages on e-mail.

Anne : Do you have my e-mail address?

Jimmy : Yes, I have your e-mail address.

Anne : All right! I look forward to hearing from you soon.
I wish you always have good luck.

Dialogue 3. There are plenty of fish in the sea.

Dolly : Hi, I haven't seen you for a while?
How is your friend, Cathy?

Jimmy : We're not seeing each other any more.

Dolly : Why? What happened?
Did you break up?

Jimmy : Yeah. I got sick and tired of her nagging all the time.

Dolly : Sorry. Maybe you were emotional at that moment.
Do you think you can get back together?

Jimmy : I don't know. There are plenty of fish in the sea.

Dolly : No. You should be open-minded.
Try again. Maybe she waits for your return.

Dialogue 4. Thanks for your advice.

Julian : What are you going to do after you graduate?

Sonya : Well, I'm preparing for the national civil service exam.
I'd like to work in social welfare. How about you?

Julian : I'm going to apply for several tourist agencies.
I want to be a tourist guide.

Sonya : I think you studied a lot about the position.

Julian : Right. But how do I apply for the position?

Sonya : You can go to the career placement officers.
The counselors at school will help you.

Julian : Thank you for the information.

Dialogue 5. You need a break for the time being.

Cathy : You have been working so hard.
You should take a vacation.
Even one or two days would be fine.

Donald : There's no way. I have too much work recently.

Cathy : But you look so exhausted. You need a break for the time being.

Donald : I know. Thanks for your understanding.
We need to hire more people but they don't.

Cathy : I see. They won't hire more people. Right?

Donald : Yeah. They always want to keep the cost down.

Cathy : Why don't you talk to the manager?
They should have some solution.

Donald : Right. I'm going to talk about it at the staff meeting.

Dialogue 6. It's not easy to meet people.

Philip : I received a letter from one of my high school friends.

Sarah : That's nice. How nice you are!

Philip : Actually I haven't heard from him in ages.

Sarah : In my case, I've been out of touch with most of my old friends.
I only keep in touch with one or two friends.

Philip : I know. It's not easy to meet people.
It's really hard to maintain contact.
People usually move around.

Sarah : That's right. People frequently move away.
But you're lucky to be in touch with your friends.

Philip : Thanks. You can try to hear from your friends.
Facebook will be helpful, I think.

Review Exercise

Write the answer to the question in English and the meaning in Korean.

1. How is your new roommate?

____.

2. What happened?

____.

3. Why don't you have a heart to heart chat with her?

____.

4. I heard you were going to move to L.A.

____.

5. Me, too. Let's keep in touch.

____.

6. Do you have my e-mail address?

____ .

7. How is your friend, Cathy?

____ .

8. Why? What happened? Did you break up?

____ .

9. Do you think you can get back together?

____ .

10. What are you going to do after you graduate?

____ .

Unit

5. Health and Care

In some cases, treatment of sick body or bad condition

Key Expressions

1. You look so bad. What's going on now?
2. I have a stomachache.
3. So what should we do now?
4. Sorry to hear that.
5. Did you have something on your mind?
6. I'm under a lot of pressure.
7. Is there anything I can do to help you?
8. Take care of yourself and cheer up.
9. What happened to your skin? On your arm.
10. Nothing serious really.
11. Who knew that a dog would cause so damage?
12. You'd better take a rest today.

Dialogue 1. I have a stomachache.

Connie : You look so bad. What's going on now?

Daniel : I have a stomachache.
I think I got some bad food at lunch today.

Connie : Really? But we ate at the same place and food.
My stomach is fine.

Daniel : You have an iron stomach.
My stomach isn't strong as you think.

Connie : So what should we do now?

Daniel : I've got to go to a clinic and see a doctor.
They will relieve my stomachache.

Dialogue 2. Maybe I can help you.

Sophie : You look so pale. What happened?

Steve : I didn't sleep a wink last night.

Sophie : Sorry to hear that.
Did you have something on your mind?

Steve : I have some problems at my office.

Sophie : You look so worried.
Tell me. Maybe I can help you.

Steve : Well, recently I'm under a lot of pressure.
My boss is very pushy. He assigned me much project.

Sophie : Um ... You are under a lot of pressure.
Is there anything I can do to help you?

Steve : Well, I guess no one can help my project.
But I just need someone to talk to.
It can relieve my stress.

Sophie : Take care of yourself and cheer up.

Dialogue 3. What did the doctor say?

John : What happened to your skin? On your arm.

Hillary : Nothing serious really.
I went to hold my dog yesterday.
When I approached it, the fingernails scrapped my arm.

John : That sounds painful.

Hillary : It wasn't bad at first, but today morning it really hurts.

John : What did the doctor say?

Hillary : He said that it should be OK.
But there might be a little scar over my skin.

John : I'm sorry to hear that.

Hillary : Thanks for your concern.
Who knew that a dog would cause so much damage?

John : Anyway you need some ointment on the skin.

Dialogue 4. Health is the most important.

Cathy : What's wrong with you? You don't look good.

David : My head is spinning, and I have a sore throat.

Cathy : Let me see. Hmm, you'd better take a rest today.
And don't work on the computer.
Staying up late with that thing has hurt your health.

David : I can't help it, but I need to use the Internet.
I should search for a lot of materials to do my report.

Cathy : I think you need to keep yourself in good shape.
Health is the most important.

David : How can I do my report? It's urgent.

Cathy : Anyway you'd better quit the internet.

Dialogue 5. I got a cold last week.

Doctor : Good afternoon. How are you feeling?

Sam : I feel horrible. I got a cold last week.
It seems to be getting worse.

Doctor : Well, let me take a listen to your chest.
Deep breath in ... and exhale.
One more again, inhale ... and exhale.

Sam : Do you hear anything interesting?

Doctor : It sounds like you have some congestion in your lungs.
Here is a prescription.

Sam : What's it for?

Doctor : It'll calm your cough.
I want you to take it two times for three days.

Sam : Yes. I should.

Doctor : And don't forget to drink lots of hot fluids.

Sam : You got it. Thank you.

Doctor : You're welcome. Take care.

Dialogue 6. Did you get burned?

Margaret : How was your time at the beach?

Phil : It was a great time there.
I really enjoyed making sand castles.

Margaret : When did you come home?

Phil : We got home about 6:00.
We spent about 6 hours there.

Margaret : That's a long time. Did you get burned?

Phil : No, I didn't. But my friends turn brown.
They should put sunscreen on.

Margaret : We must protect our skin from the sun.

Review Exercise

Write the answer to the question in English and the meaning in Korean.

1. You look so bad. What's going on now?

____.

2. My stomach is fine.

____.

3. So what should we do now?

____.

4. You look so pale. What happened?

____.

5. Did you have something on your mind?

____.

6. Tell me. Maybe I can help you.

____.

7. Is there anything I can do to help you?

____.

8. What happened to your skin? On your arm.

____.

9. What did the doctor say?

____.

10. Who knew that a dog would cause so damage?

____.

Unit 6. Housing and Facilities

Expressions of indoor and outdoor facilities

Key Expressions

1. Has your friend moved out?
2. It's still worth of the burden, isn't it?
3. If I had a chance, I would move out here.
4. You must be roasting.
5. You must be kidding me.
6. I can stand the hot weather.
7. The warmer, the better.
8. To tell the truth, I also feel uncomfortable.
9. Hello, is this a maintenance office?
10. What problems do you have?
11. You're going to have a big problem.
12. I must go out now. I have an appointment in thirty minutes.

Dialogue 1. Has your friend moved out?

Mark : Has your friend moved out?

Karen : Yes. He moved out last week.
He's living in a very quiet apartment.

Mark : I wonder why he's paying more for rent.
That is a big burden.

Karen : I agree, but I have a different idea.
It's still worth of burden, isn't it?

Mark : You're right. He had a good choice.
I think he's probably glad to leave that noisy apartment.

Karen : Yes, he sure is.
If I had a chance, I would move out here.

Dialogue 2. The warmer, the better.

John : It's very hot. It's like a melting pot here.
You must be roasting.

Margaret : Actually, I don't care. I'm comfortable.

John : You must be kidding me.
It may be over 30 degrees here.

Margaret : I can stand the hot weather.
The warmer, the better.

John : You are strong-willed person, aren't you?

Margaret : To tell the truth, I also feel uncomfortable.

John : Well. Can we open a window and get some ventilation?

Margaret : You go ahead.

John : Thanks. I will.

Dialogue 3. I have a problem in my room.

Dolly : Hello, is this a maintenance office?

Julius : Yes, this is the office.

Dolly : This is the tenant of this apartment.
My room number is 312.
I have some problems in my room.

Julius : What problems do you have?

Dolly : My kitchen sink is clogged up again.
And so is the bathtub.

Julius : All right, I'll send someone this afternoon.

Dolly : Thanks. But I want you to send someone now.
I can't cook.
I can't take a shower.

Julius : Oh, that's terrible. I'll be up in a few minutes.

Dolly : Thanks. I appreciate it.

Dialogue 4. The water faucet is dripping again.

Estella : Oh, no! The water faucet is dripping again.

Ben : That's terrible. You have a big problem.

Estella : Yes. I must fix it as soon as possible.

Ben : Don't you want to fix it now?

Estella : I wish I could, but I can't now.

Ben : Why? What's wrong?

Estella : I must go out now. I have an appointment in thirty minutes.

Ben : Well, if you need anything, just let me know.

Estella : Can you give me a ride? My car is still in the service center.

Ben : Yes, I can help you.

Dialogue 5. The cafe has a strong air-conditioner.

Donald : Don't you have air-conditioning in your apartment?
It's hot everyday.

Alice : Umm ..., There's air-conditioning.
Did you see that air-conditioner on the corner?
The air-conditioner is not powerful enough.

Donald : I guess so. That's a big problem.

Alice : Well, we should move out anyway.
The cafe has a strong air-conditioner.

Donald : Yes, we can stay there over some coffee.

Alice : Many people stay in the cafe to avoid the hot weather.

Donald : Sure. How can we stand the heat without air-conditioning?

Alice : Hurry to go there.

Dialogue 6. Did you call the apartment manager?

Grace : I turned on the faucet, but there was no water coming out.
Can you help me with this problem?

Henry : Sorry to hear that. Is there not a single drop?

Grace : Well, there is just drip, drip, drip.
I need to use a lot of water at the moment.

Henry : Did you call the apartment manager?

Grace : Yes. I called this morning and noticed it.
They said they would send someone over to my apartment.

Henry : But they must come soon. Right?

Grace : Yes, but they said they would be busy.
They will come here in the afternoon.

Review Exercise

Write the answer to the question in English and the meaning in Korean.

1. Has your friend moved out?

____.

2. I wonder he's paying more for rent. That is a big burden.

____.

3. It's still worth of the burden, isn't it?

____.

4. It's very hot. It's like a melting pot here.

____.

5. You must be kidding me. It may be over 30 degrees here.

____.

6. You are strong-willed person, aren't you?

____ .

7. Well. Can we open a window and get some ventilation?

____ .

8. Hello, is this a maintenance office?

____ .

9. What problems do you have?

____ .

10. I'll send someone this afternoon.

____ .

Part II

Speaking Skill (의사 표현 능력)

Unit

7. Memory and Experience

Something to memorize, especially in the present or past

Key Expressions

1. Do you know Jimmy's phone number?
2. That's too bad. I've got to find his number.
3. I've tried some friends, but no one answered.
4. I will find his number as soon as I get home
5. I heard you're going to take a test.
6. There shouldn't be any problems.
7. We finally have a wonderful vacation.
8. I hope it's nothing serious.
9. It's just something personal.
10. What should we do now?
11. Do you have anything in mind?
12. I'll make a phone call.

Dialogue 1. She has his phone number.

Bernard : Do you know Jimmy's phone number?

Connie : Oh, his phone number?
I don't have my address book on me.
I can't think of it right now.

Bernard : That's too bad. I've got to find his number.
I have to contact him.
It's urgent. I must contact him today.

Connie : Well, why don't you call Grace?
She has his phone number.

Bernard : I've tried some friends, but no one answered.

Connie : Oh, you are so dead.
I will find his number as soon as I get home.

Dialogue 2. The traffic rules are confusing.

Sandra : I heard you're going to take a test.
Is it for the driver's license test?

Allen : Yeah. I will do that this week.

Sandra : You've been studying the test for weeks.
There shouldn't be any problems.

Allen : But I still need to memorize some traffic rules.
The traffic rules are confusing.
Some rules are hard to tell the differences.

Sandra : You'll be fine. Just use the guidebook.

Allen : Yeah, but sometimes the signs are also confusing.

Dialogue 3. It's just something personal.

Anne : We finally have a wonderful vacation.
First, we will go to the concert hall this Friday.
Are you coming with us?

Alex : I wish I could, but something unexpected has come up.

Anne : I see. You look so concerned.
I hope it's nothing serious.

Alex : Well, it's just something personal.

Anne : OK. But if you need help, let me know.

Alex : Sure. I will. You are so kind.

Dialogue 4. I forgot to invite her.

Matthew : I sent out the invitations for my birthday party.

Lillian : That's good. What should we do now?

Matthew : We should plan the menu.

Lillian : Do you have anything in mind?

Matthew : I think I'm going to make the chicken salad.
I know the recipe.

Lillian : But my friend Grace doesn't eat chicken.

Matthew : Grace? Oh, my god! I forgot to invite her.
That’s my mistake.

Lillian : Well, it's not too late yet. I'll make a phone call.
Don't worry.

Matthew : Thanks. I sometimes forget important things.

Lillian : Don't worry. Everybody makes a mistake.

Dialogue 5. She answers that it's privacy.

Allen : Do you know what Andy's phone number is?

Grace : I can't think of it in my head.
You can look it up in your phone address.

Allen : I've checked it.
His phone number is unlisted or erased.

Grace : Maybe it's under the group of classmate's names.

Allen : Well, I guess so.

Grace : Or you can call his office and ask his secretary.

Allen : I've already tried, but she won't tell me.
She answers that it's privacy.

Grace : Oh, that's right.
They don't release private information to others.

Allen : Yes. Recently privacy is important.

Dialogue 6. I will buy a new watch.

Jason : My watch always gains about five minutes a day.

Mary : That's funny.
My watch always loses five minutes a day.

Jason : No kidding.

Mary : I'm serious.
Every morning I set my watch by the radio or TV.
But it still loses five minutes.

Jason : Do you know what we can do?

Mary : Can we fix it? Or can we buy a new one?

Jason : Right. That's what I'm doing.

Mary : Why bother?
I will buy a new watch. It doesn't cost much.
I can't stand this thing any more.

Review Exercise

Write the answer to the question in English and the meaning in Korean.

1. Do you know Jimmy's phone number?

____ .

2. I have something to contact him. I must contact him today.

____ .

3. I've tried some friends, but no one answered.

____ .

4. I heard you're going to take a test. Is it for driver's license test?

____ .

5. Some rules are hard to tell the differences.

____ .

6. Are you coming with us?

____.

7. Sure. I will. You are so kind.

____.

8. That's good. What should we do now?

____.

9. Oh, that's right. Do you have anything in mind?

____.

10. Yeah, my friend Grace doesn't eat chicken.

____.

Unit 8. Shopping

Purchasing in a shopping center or a department store

Key Expressions

1. How much did you pay for it?
2. That's a rip-off.
3. It's too expensive. It's not worth it.
4. I really did get ripped off.
5. I shouldn't have bought it.
6. I'd love to, but I'm broke.
7. I like browsing through the store.
8. Actually, I'm broke.
9. We can do window shopping, can't we?
10. Just looking around? No, that's boring.
11. Is there anything else you would like to buy?
12. Keep your receipt.

Dialogue 1. It's too expensive.

Allen : How much did you pay for it?

Dolly : It's 250 dollars.

Allen : You paid 250 dollars for a smart-phone like that.
That's a rip-off.

Dolly : What do you mean?

Allen : It's a piece of junk, I think.
It's too expensive. It's not worth it.

Dolly : I see. I really did get ripped off.
I shouldn't have bought it.

Allen : Next time, I will follow you at shopping.

Dolly : Good advice. I am sure.

Dialogue 2. I like browsing through the store.

Sam : Do you want to come to the mall with me?

Mary : I'd love to, but I'm broke.

Sam : So am I, but I like browsing through the store.

Mary : Are you sure you only want to browse?

Sam : Yes. I like to look around there.

Mary : I don't have money to buy them.

Sam : I know but we can go there and see something.

Mary : Great. Let's go there and try on something.

Dialogue 3. We can go window shopping.

Issac : Sunny Shopping Mall is having a big sale this weekend.
Do you want to go with me?

Mary : I'd love to but I don't feel like it.
Actually, I'm broke.

Issac : Well, we can go window shopping, can't we?
I want to spend some time there to browse.

Mary : Just looking around? No, that's boring.

Issac : They serve free samples.
I will try some pieces of food for free.

Mary : Is it true? That's interesting.
I will go with you. Let's drop by there.

Issac : Hurry up. Let's go.

Dialogue 4. Keep the receipt.

Cashier : Is there anything else?

Jimmy : Excuse me?

Cashier : Is there anything else you would like to buy?

Jimmy : No, thank you. I think that's all.

Cashier : Anything for help?

Jimmy : Can I return it if it has any problems?

Cashier : Yes. But you must return it within two weeks.

Jimmy : Yes, I see.

Cashier : Keep your receipt.
If something comes up, you can show it to us.
And we'll give you a refund.

Jimmy : Thanks.

Dialogue 5. Do you take credit cards?

Steve : Excuse me.

Waitress : Yes. How was everything? Did you enjoy this food here?

Steve : Really nice. Thank you.

Waitress : Would you like this to take out?

Steve : Yes, I want it to take out. Can you put it in a plastic bag?

Waitress : Sure. No problem. Wait a minute.

Steve : Thank you. And how much is it?

Waitress : That will be 120 dollars.

Steve : Do you take a credit card?

Waitress : Yes, we accept it.

Steve : OK, here you are.

Waitress : Here's your receipt. Please come again.

Steve : Thank you. See you.

Dialogue 6. Is it possible to get a discount?

Clerk : Hello. Are you being helped?

Karen : I'm interested in some blouses.

Clerk : All our blouses are in this section.
What do you think of this one here?
It's made of silk.

Karen : I think that's what I want. How much is it?

Clerk : It's sixty-five dollars.

Karen : It's a little expensive, I think.
Is it possible to get a discount?

Clerk : How about 10 percent discount?

Karen : That's good. I will get it.
Could you wrap it up for me?

Clerk : Sure.

Review Exercise

Write the answer to the question in English and the meaning in Korean.

1. How much did you pay for it?

____.

2. What do you mean?

____.

3. I see. I really did get ripped off. I shouldn't have bought it.

____.

4. Do you want to come to the mall with me?

____.

5. Are you sure you only want to browse?

____.

6. I don't have money to buy them.

____ .

7. Do you want to go with me?

____ .

8. I want to browse there and spend time.

____ .

9. I will try on some pieces of food for free.

____ .

10. Let's drop there.

____ .

Unit

9. Traffic Problems

Automobile problems to fix and traffics on the street

Key Expressions

1. I must find someone to fix it for me.
2. Maybe you should change a new battery.
3. Anyway I'm going to return it.
4. Why didn't you send a message?
5. I'm sorry. I couldn't help it.
6. He was taken to the hospital.
7. I hope he will recover soon.
8. You turned on the red light.
9. You should not turn on red.
10. May I see your driver's license or insurance policy?
11. I have to give you a ticket.
12. You can't park here.

Dialogue 1. Did you check the battery first?

Emily : My car did not start this morning.

Kevin : I sometimes have the same problem.
Did you check the battery first?

Emily : Yes. It was dead again.
I must find someone to fix it for me.
In this case, it makes me crazy.

Kevin : Well, maybe you should replace a battery.

Emily : But I bought this one six months ago.
It's still new, I think.

Kevin : Maybe the battery is wrong.

Emily : Anyway I'm going to return it.
I will go to the service center.

Dialogue 2. Fortunately he wasn't hurt badly.

Cathy : Why didn't you show up for the meeting?
All other friends were a little upset.

Allen : I know. I'm awfully sorry.

Cathy : Why didn't you send a message?
Did you have any emergency?

Allen : I'm sorry. I couldn't help it.
My brother had an accident. He was hit by a car.
He was taken to the hospital.

Cathy : Oh, that's too bad. Is he OK?

Allen : Fortunately he wasn't hurt badly.
But the skin of an arm was damaged.

Cathy : I hope he will recover soon.

Dialogue 3. May I see your driver's license?

Officer : Excuse me, ma'am. Didn't you see the red light?
You turned on the red light.

Olive : Oh, I thought I could make a right turn on red here.

Officer : No, ma'am. The sign says "No Turn on Red."
You should not turn on red.

Olive : Oh, I guess I didn't see it.

Officer : I'm sorry, ma'am.
May I see your driver's license or insurance policy?
I have to give you a ticket.

Olive : Here they are, sir.

Officer : Sign here, please.
You can appeal to the court within 14 days.
Please drive safely, ma'am.

Olive : Thank you, sir.

Dialogue 4. You can't park here.

Officer : Excuse me, ma'am. You can't park here.

Rose : I'm just waiting for my friends here.
It won't be long.
Is there any problem to park here?

Officer : Ma'am, the curb here is not for parking.

Rose : But I didn't see the sign, sir.

Officer : There's a sign at the corner of the street.
When you turned in here, you should have seen it.

Rose : That's too bad. I didn't see it.

Officer : I'm sorry, ma'am. I have to give you a ticket.
You can appeal to the court within 14 days.

Dialogue 5. Did you find any other route?

Amelia : Oh, my god! The traffic is crawling there.

Max : I think there's a traffic accident ahead.

Amelia : We're now running late.

Max : I know. Why don't we take a different route?

Amelia : Let me take a look at the map.

Max : Did you find any other route?

Amelia : Yes, there's an exit two miles ahead.
We'll exit other next street, and then get on the other road.

Max : OK, let's take the road.

Amelia : But we may take a longer way.

Max : It doesn't matter. That's a shortcut.

Dialogue 6. We will have a traffic problem.

Stella : I heard you are going to the airport in the evening.

Jason : Yes. I am. I will have a meeting with my group there.

Stella : Well, you may not know this. It's Friday today.
So, everybody stops work early in the afternoon.

Jason : Do you mean we will have a traffic problem?

Stella : That's right. Today they go back home early.

Jason : How will it be?

Stella : Traffic usually becomes very busy in the afternoon.

Jason : I didn't think about it.
I must leave a little early today.

Stella : Leave as early as possible.
You'd better hurry up in the afternoon.

Jason : I see.

Review Exercise

Write the answer to the question in English and the meaning in Korean.

1. Did you check the battery first?

____.

2. In this case, it's driving me crazy.

____.

3. But I bought this one six months ago. It's still new, I think.

____.

4. Why didn't you show up for the meeting yesterday?

____.

5. Did you have any emergency problem?

____.

6. Oh, that's too bad. Is he OK?

____ .

7. Excuse me, ma'am. Didn't you see the red light?

____ .

8. You should not turned on red.

____ .

9. May I see your driver's license or insurance policy?

____ .

10. Please drive safely, ma'am.

____ .

Unit 10. Traveling

Traveling guide and the places to see or look around

Key Expressions

1. Excuse me. Can you do me a favor?
2. Can you keep an eye on my bag, please?
3. I just want to use the bathroom.
4. Where did you leave it?
5. Have you checked it again?
6. You should have kept an eye on it.
7. What can I do for you?
8. Can you save my place for me, please?
9. I see. It won't be long. I'll be right back.
10. I'd like to make a reservation.
11. What kind of rooms do you have?
12. How many nights will you stay?

Dialogue 1. When will you be back?

Tom : Excuse me. Can you do me a favor?

Anne : Sure. What is it?

Tom : Can you keep an eye on my bag, please?
I want to go out there for a minute.

Anne : Sure. When will you be back?
I will take the next train within 30 minutes.
Will you be long?

Tom : No. I just want to use the bathroom.
I will be back soon.

Anne : Go ahead. It'll be safe with me.

Dialogue 2. I guess someone stole it.

Harry : Where is my backpack?

Sara : I don't know. I can't see it anywhere.
Where did you leave it?

Harry : I just put it on the chair a few minutes ago.
It should be here on the chair.
But now it's gone. It's strange.

Sara : Are you sure?
Have you checked it again?

Harry : Of course, I'm sure. I bet someone took it.
In other words, I guess someone stole it.

Sara : You should have kept an eye on it.
You made a mistake.

Dialogue 3. The line is moving fast.

Maria : Excuse me. Can you do me a favor?

Tim : Sure. What is it?
What can I do for you?

Maria : Can you save my place for me, please?
I will buy some drinks. I will come back soon.

Tim : Sure. But hurry. The line is moving fast, I think.
I will keep your place.

Maria : And I will drop by the restroom on the way.

Tim : Yeah, but don't take too long.
I'm afraid people might complain about it.
Anyway, don't worry. I will keep your place.

Maria : I see. It won't be long.
I'll be right back.

Dialogue 4. What kind of rooms do you have?

Clerk : Good evening, sir. May I help you?

Adams : Yes. I'd like to make a reservation.
What kind of rooms do you have?

Clerk : We have some vacancies.
How large is your party?

Adams : Three. Two adults and one child.

Clerk : Let see, we have a room with two double beds.
How many nights will you stay?

Adams : Just one night. We're only staying overnight.

Clerk : I see. You are booked for one night, two adults and one child.
Have a good time.

Dialogue 5. I had a lot of time on the beach.

Alex : How was your vacation?

Dolly : Oh, it was great! I had a great time on the beach.

Alex : It sounds wonderful. You're so dark.

Dolly : Yeah. I had a lot of time on the beach.

Alex : What else did you do?

Dolly : Nothing special. It was good just to relax.

Alex : I wish I could get away like you.

Dolly : Really? I will invite you next time.

Alex : Thanks. I really envy you.

Dialogue 6. May I sit here?

Kate : Excuse me. Is this seat taken?

Sam : I'm sorry. What did you say?

Kate : Oh. Will someone be using this seat?
May I sit here?

Sam : No, it's a vacant seat. You can take it.

Kate : Thanks.

Sam : Which side would you like, an aisle or a window?

Kate : I want to sit on the aisle side.
Would you mind moving to the window, please?

Sam : No, not at all.

Review Exercise

Write the answer to the question in English and the meaning in Korean.

1. Excuse me. Can you do me a favor?

____.

2. Can you keep an eye on my bag, please?

____.

3. Will you be long?

____

4. Where is my backpack?

____.

5. Where did you leave it?

____.

6. Are you sure? Have you checked it again?

____.

7. Excuse me. Can you do me a favor?

____.

8. Can you save my place for me, please?

____.

9. And I will drop by the restroom on the way.

____.

10. Anyway, don't worry. I will keep your place.

____.

Unit

11. Vacation or Holiday

Special days to relax or to take a rest after work

Key Expressions

1. What date is it today?
2. I'm leaving on Friday. We're going to Africa.
3. How long are you going to stay there?
4. When are you coming back?
5. I don't have any classes now.
6. What do you plan to do?
7. You'd better go out of your place.
8. I wish I could, but I don't have enough money.
9. Why? Has something come up?
10. I've got to talk about it with my husband.
11. I really appreciate your understanding.
12. What else did you do?

Dialogue 1. Great. Have a nice trip.

George : What date is it today?

Sandra : It's July 7th.

George : When are you going on vacation?

Sandra : I'm leaving on Friday. We're going to Africa.

George : Really? The day after tomorrow? That's very soon.

Sandra : Yes, I know.

George : How long are you going to stay there?

Sandra : About 3 weeks.

George : When are you coming back?

Sandra : I'm coming back on the 5th of next month.

George : Great. Have a nice trip.

Dialogue 2. You'd better go out of your place.

Jack : Do you have school today?

Lisa : No, I don't have any classes now.
This semester has finished.

Jack : Really? What do you plan to do?

Lisa : Well, I don't know what I'm going to do with my free time.

Jack : Are you planning to take any summer classes?
You said you would study hard during vacation.

Lisa : No. I think I'll just relax.
I have studied hard for this semester.
So I need a break. Only a long break.

Jack : You'd better go out of your place.
Why don't you go to the resort to take a full rest?

Lisa : I wish I could, but I don't have enough money.

Dialogue 3. You need a family vacation this time.

Gloria : When are you going to take your vacation?

Nick : I am planning to take it at the end of next month.

Gloria : You need a family vacation this time.

Nick : Yes. We are planning to travel to the South Pacific. However, I have a problem.

Gloria : Why? Has something come up?

Nick : Could you change your working schedule for me?

Gloria : Umm .... I've got to talk about it with my husband. He will understand it. It may be no problem.

Nick : I really appreciate your understanding. Thank you very much.

Dialogue 4. How was your vacation?

Gilbert : How was your vacation?

Cathy : Oh, it was great. I had a great time on the beach.

Gilbert : No wonder you're so dark.

Cathy : Yeah. I had a lot of time to work on my tan.

Gilbert : What else did you do?

Cathy : Nothing. It was good just to relax.

Gilbert : I wish I could get away like that. It sounds wonderful.

Cathy : Did you say you're going to take a vacation next week?

Gilbert : Yes. I'm going to South Asia for a week.

Cathy : I really envy you.
I wish I could get away for a while again.

Dialogue 5. Do you have any plans?

Tina : I'm so glad. I finally have a long weekend.

Daniel : We've got a vacation for two weeks.
It's an exciting time.

Tina : Where're you going?

Daniel : I don't have any plans yet.
Well, I make to the USA.
How about you?
Do you have any plans?

Tina : I'm going to go to South Asia with my family.

Daniel : That sounds exciting.

Tina : How long will you be there?

Daniel : Maybe four or five days. Less than a week.

Tina : I envy you. I hope to go there later.

Dialogue 6. I went on a trip last week.

Sophie : Hi. How have you been lately?

David : I went on a trip last week.

Sophie : Really? Where did you go?

David : We went to the USA.

Sophie : What cities did you go to?

David : New York, Washington. DC., and a few other smaller cities.

Sophie : Did you go to Alaska?

David : No, I didn't go there. I'd like to go there next time.

Sophie : I think the summer is a good time to visit Alaska.
It's a beautiful place and the people there are very nice.

David : That's what I've heard.

Sophie : I went there last year.
I can give you some information about the state.

David : Thanks.

Review Exercise

Write the answer to the question in English and the meaning in Korean.

1. What date is it today?

____.

2. When are you going on vacation?

____.

3. How long are you going to stay there?

____.

4. When are you coming back?

____.

5. Do you have school today?

____.

6. Really? What do you plan to do?

____ .

7. Are you planning to take any summer classes?

____ .

8. Why don't you go to the resort to take a full rest?

____ .

9. When are you going to take your vacation?

____ .

10. You need a family vacation this time.

____ .

Unit 12. Weather

Temperature, cold or hot, and other expressions to mention weather

Key Expressions

1. I've never seen such hot weather in my life.
2. I guess so. What else can we do?
3. How's the weather there today?
4. What's the temperature?
5. I don't like the winter. I wish it were spring.
6. Nobody can stand it.
7. You should hear my advice.
8. Didn't you turn on the air-conditioner?
9. The air-conditioner doesn't work any more.
10. How can we stay here?
11. What's going on?
12. I guess the pipes are frozen again.

Dialogue 1. It's really hot everywhere.

Charles : Oh, my god. It's really hot everywhere.
I've never seen such hot weather in my life.

Hillary : It's like the whole world is boiling.

Charles : Why not? Look at the thermometer.
The temperature has hit already 30 degrees Celsius.

Hillary : It will go up more in the afternoon.

Charles : But it's already close.

Hillary : Well, I hope it'll stop the point now.

Charles : I guess we can't do anything until after dark.

Hillary : I guess so. What else can we do?
We can't stay in the heat for long.

Dialogue 2. What's the temperature?

Tina : Hello.

Gilbert : Hi. How's the weather there today?

Tina : It's cold. It snowed all day and the schools closed today.

Gilbert : What's the temperature?

Tina : It's 15 degrees below now. It was even colder this morning.

Gilbert : Have you heard what the weather will be like tomorrow?

Tina : I was watching the news.
They said it's probably going to snow tomorrow.

Gilbert : I don't like the winter. I wish it were spring.

Tina : Me too. How's the weather where you are?

Gilbert : It's pretty cold here too.
It's going to be a little colder tomorrow.

Dialogue 3. We must drink a lot of fluids.

Kathy : Oh, my god. We can't stand this kind of hot heat.

Adam : Right. Nobody can stand it.
We can't stay outside for one minute.

Kathy : Sure. It's dangerous to go out, isn't it?

Adam : Anyway, there's nothing we can do.
Everybody should stay inside the building.

Kathy : I guess so.
Some people are taken to the hospital for heat exhaustion.
And sunstroke is also dangerous.

Adam : You should hear my advice.
Drink a lot of liquids and avoid the heat.

Kathy : You're right. We must drink a lot of fluids.

Dialogue 4. I can't stand the heat here.

Cony : Oh, the heat is unbearable today.
Didn't you turn on the air-conditioner?

Paul : The heat has blown off everything.
I have turned on the air-conditioner all day long.
Now the air-conditioner doesn't work any more.

Cony : What? So, what are we going to do?

Paul : We've got to have it fixed as soon as possible.
I've called someone to fix it. And they're on the way.

Cony : Oh, my god. How can we stay here?
I can't stand the heat here.

Paul : You can use the electric fan here. Here you go.
At least you can catch a breeze.

Dialogue 5. I guess the pipes are frozen again.

Nick : What's going on?

Sandra : When I turn on the faucet, it's just drip, drip, drip.
Well, it's the second day in a row.

Nick : I guess the pipes are frozen again.

Sandra : Really? Then how can I wash?
Where should I go?

Nick : Yesterday the water went off without warning.
I couldn't take a shower.
And I couldn't wash the dishes.

Sandra : Well, I'm wondering why the manager didn't show up.
We should find out any places to wash.

Dialogue 6. We didn't have rain this month.

Sally : I guess a drought has come in.
It hasn't rained a drop for months.

Matthew : I think so, too. We didn't have rain this month.

Sally : It did rain last month.
The rainfall was less than half the monthly average.

Matthew : Oh. That's too bad.

Sally : It's a really bad season.
I'm worried about the agriculture in the field.

Matthew : The fruits and vegetables do not grow any more.

Sally : Right. The soil has been baked so hard.
But a lot of plants do not grow on the brown soil.

Matthew : Yeah. If it doesn't rain, it's critical.

Review Exercise

Write the answer to the question in English and the meaning in Korean.

1. I've never seen such hot weather in my life.

____ .

2. The temperature has hit already 30 degrees Celsius.

____ .

3. But it's already awfully close.

____ .

4. I guess we can't do anything until after dark.

____ .

5. Hi. How's the weather there today?

____ .

6. What's the temperature?

____.

7. Have you heard what the weather will be like tomorrow?

____.

8. How's the weather where you are?

____.

9. We can't stand this kind of hot heat, can we?

____.

10. Sure. It's dangerous to go out, isn't it?

____.

Part III

Reading Skill (문서 이해 능력)

- Self-introduction Letter (1)
- Self-introduction Letter (2)
- Business Letter (1)
- Business Letter (2)
- Business Letter (3)
- Business Letter (4)
- Business Letter (5)
- A Letter of Recommendation 1 (추천서 1)
- A Letter of Recommendation 2 (추천서 2)
- A Letter of Recommendation 3 (추천서 3)

Self-introduction Letter (1)

Self-introduction Letter

My name is Black Stone. From now, I will introduce myself from a young girl to a lady like now. I was born in 1996 and I am 21 years old. I was born in Seoul, Korea. Now I live in an apartment near the Stone University, L.A.

I grew up in the village and that's why I have been very healthy until now. I was raised like other normal kids with my loved family. I have gracious parents and a kind old brother. I am always proud of my family. My family is the source of my energy and the goal of my life.

After I finished the middle school in the village, I entered the high school in town. The school was famous for the good teachers and the students studying there had entered high rated colleges or universities. I studied hard every day and I got a good grade during the school. Furthermore, I had a wonderful time and experience in my favorite high school for 3 years.

My dreams came true after the high school. I entered a university and I expected to have a lot of freedom. For one year as a freshman, I did almost everything. I couldn't get good grades for the first year in the university, but I made precious friends and met people around myself.

I have lots of hobbies and activities. I sometimes go hiking with my club members. I usually exercise about four hours a week, and I like to go to the movie. I like swimming, baseball, and table tennis.

My major is international relationship. After I graduate from the university, I will apply for a company in the field where I have been studying. I thought that I needed to improve my English. So I did my best in studying English and got certificates in English. I'll try to do my best in the field of my major.

Write a self-introduction letter including your future plans.

Self-introduction Letter (2)

Self-introduction

I am very glad to have a chance to introduce myself to you. I am in the 1st grade in the Department of High-Tech Industry of the Blackstone University. I was born as an elder sister with one brother, and my parents believe that faith and honesty are more valuable than any other else. We could talk about anything with love. My father always taught us love, responsibility, independence, and so on.

On the other hand, my mother always taught me to have endurance and peace of mind. I think that my mother's lesson was the afformative attitude in life. I can't forget that my mother woke me up early in the morning and she used to read a book by my bed. She usually taught me something important in studying.

When I was in the high school, I was an active student in school or out of school life. I think that I had a strong leadership as a president of my class. My class loved me very much. That is, they liked my kindness and strong leadership. I think that I received something valuable from them in my school life. When I had difficulty in the class, my afformative attitude would help me a lot, which was one of my merits from my father.

My present goal is to become a woman engineer in the future after graduating from my university. I have won the prize on math and science contests when I was in the elementary and the middle school. Those experiences are helpful for my future, and I will try to do my best to get another dream. I think that I am lucky in Black University because I can make my dream come true someday.

Nowadays I joined the student club that I wanted. I had another world with the club in my university. The seniors in the club suggest that I should study hard and be active in the life of university. They say that foreign language classes are very important for students. My seniors, my friends, and my professors help me get my goal as a woman engineer in the future.

Write a self-introduction letter including your future plans.

Business Letter (1)

August 24, 2007

Jimmy Shim, Ph. D
1300-1003 Gaenari Apt. Sanbon-dong
Gunpo, Gyunggi-do 435-768, South Korea

Dear Consular Officer,

This is an official invitation for Jimmy Shim to present "The lexical decision of the native and foreign language: the effects of age on reaction time and functional MRI study" at Neuroscience 2007, November 3-7, 2007 in San Diego, CA.

The Society for Neuroscience (SfN) is a nonprofit membership organization of basic scientists and physicians who study the brain and nervous system. The Society's primary goal is to promote the exchange of information among researchers. For this purpose, SfN holds a prestigious annual meeting, attended by scientists and researchers from around the globe. It is considered the most important annual forum for the neuroscience research community, offering attendees the opportunity to learn about the latest advances in brain research. Also we expect to meet and network with their colleagues at top destinations throughout the United States.

This invitation does not include any financial support for your travel, registration fees, or local expenses once you arrive at the meeting.

Sincerely,

Lillian Bathman

Lillian Bathman, Ph. D
Director of Annual Meeting Program Department
Society for Neuroscience

Business Letter (2)

May 24, 2010

Dear Ms. Sophia Chen,

Thank you for your email. We have had some meetings for your requirements. We have talked about the problems that you asked, especially for incentive scheme. I am really sorry for my late answer, for we have reviewed your scheme again during the national holiday, the Buddhist Day. Please review the following scheme that we have decided.

Incentive Scheme

Test/Month	Cost (USD)	Amount (USD)	Bonus (%)
300	41.5	12,450	9 tests (3%)
500	40	20,000	25 tests (5%)
1,000	38	38,000	70 tests (7%)
2,000	35	70,000	160 tests (8%)
3,000	30	90,000	300 tests (10%)

The MediNex was established on the 10th of October, 1998 and developed the hair test technique for our own technology supported by the Korean government. We also developed the analysis method and dissolution food for hard ware. The product has been sold since the 1st of October, 2001.

I will send the contract letter as soon as the initial form on the content of Asia and China is finished. I thank and wait for your further inquires soon.

Yours sincerely,

Sunkwan Kim

Sunkwan Kim
Commercial Director of the MediNex

Business Letter (3)

RE : S. H. Kim from Medinex Korea.
date 28 May, 2010 Friday 11: 51: 31 am
sender "Alice Chen" ⟨alicechen@yahoo.com⟩

recipient : Kim Sun Hee ⟨kimsun33@hanmail.net⟩
referent : Lee Alex ⟨kaklaka22@yahoo.com⟩

Dear Kim,

As you know, we need the time to build up the business. However, as starting the business, we need to invest a lot on the business, like what we have done in 26 of May. With the investment on the business, we will be able to increase the interests of the people.

Therefore, if at the beginning you do not do the support to us, how can we reach the big volume?

As you know, we are not just doing your hair testing. The most important problem is the supplement. Therefore, we urgently need your supplement, detail information, and the price.

We will work out the most incentive for ourselves, so let us know more information in detail in advance.

Yours truly,
Alice Chen

Write a business letter asking business promotion.

Business Letter (4)

December 12, 2015

Dear Ms. Mary Sanderson,

I notice you Mr. Jimmy Lee is a new official of trade and representative process in my company.

Our office also produced a new product, so we think you need it. We may notice you of our ingredients that you asked.

However, to get the product, they need the order form that was ordered from foreign countries. So, they asked you a temporary or an sample order though we have not had a trade yet.

In other word, they ask you a sample proving that you are an overseas trade company. You can send your sample by email with the type of company logo.

Thanks your consideration of the business.

Yours truly,

Seon-Gwan Kim

Sales Director of Medinex Korea Co., Ltd.

Write a business letter explaining business problems.

Business Letter (5)

Anne 28, 2010

Dear Dr. Alison,

I am really pleased to meet you in this letter through the introduction of Dr. Alison. My name is Mr. Kim Sun, a member of the Medicare. I am in charge of the export process of the Nutrition of Korean item.

I would like to discuss our opinion and requirements with you for the process of the business in advance.

1. Please send your INVOICE for the process.

2. With the INVOICE, I want to know how to pay the bill for the item.
   I would like to send it through L/C for our preference.

3. Please notice me your method of an import permission for the item. That is, I want to know whether you treat the process for your own or through the commission agency.

I am really appreciate for your consideration of this business.
Please send me your kind reply as soon as possible.

Yours sincerely,

Jimmy Kim

Write a business letter to introduce a new product to a customer.

A Letter of Recommendation 1 (추천서 1)

March 5, 2016

Dear sir/ma'am,

I am really pleased with the recommendation of my student, Ms. Hyesong Kim. She has already prepared for the MA. program of tourism management with a lot of trainings and experiences at the university. Her international experience and service meet the requirement of the degree program. Furthermore, she is interested in the hotel management in foreign countries where she has been working for many years. As her aim for the course is from her practical experience, she will successfully accomplish the course.

She has a quite good communicative proficiency in commanding English. Most of her training in the past has been related to the foreign countries where she speaks in English. Her international relationship with others who came from various countries will be helpful to her perspective course in Banana Tourism University.

Sincerely yours,

Jimmy Shim, Ph. D.
The head of the Department of English

A Letter of Recommendation 2 (추천서 2)

Personal Comments on the Applicant
(추천인에 대한 개인 의견)

I would like to mention the applicant's ability to relate to others. The applicant has served long periods of social welfare, especially for low class of children. She also worked as a volunteer in foreign countries. During the service in the foreign countries, her experience was directly related to others who had colorful cultures or different language backgrounds.

In my honest opinion, her sincere service was surely originated from her good relationship with others as well as her strong faith in human nature. In addition, she was a leader in managing academic discussion and volunteer activities during the university course. I am sure that other students and academic faculties have the same idea in respect to her accomplishment.

After she graduates from the MA. in social welfare, she will work in the field in Korea. Her other aim is to give service to the social welfare community.

A Letter of Recommendation 3 (추천서 3)

Personal Comments on the Character (추천인 성격에 대한 의견)

The applicant has some outstanding merits in personal characteristics and traits. First, he had quite affirmative and rational attitude to the academic approach during the course. For example, he liked discussion in the class, so he always presented interesting learning materials and topics. He discussed the questions with friends in or out of the class. The learning approach helped the course interesting and instructive for other participants in the course.

Second, he was interested in the primary or secondary education in the third world. He hoped to share his knowledge with the brothers and sisters who did not have educational chances.

Third, his ways of learning mostly focused on his deep faith in religious point of view. In other words, I guess that his purpose of learning was to intensify his belief or trust as a member of religious community.

Fourth, his command of English was almost an advanced level in four skills: listening, speaking, reading, and writing. I am sure that his English proficiency and professional knowledge on English are the basis of other courses.

To conclude, Mr. Lee will study hard the course and will finish it successfully. After the course, he will make use of his academic training for realizing public lives of others who need his help.

Memo

Part Ⅳ

Writing Skill
(문서 작성 능력)

- Sample Resume
  - (1) : Publishing Company
  - (2) : Accountant
  - (3) : Tourism and Hotel Management
  - (4) : Technical Writing and Editing
  - (5) : Business Administration
  - (6) : Tourism Business
  - (7) : Information Technology
  - (8) : Hotel
  - (9) : Financial Services
  - (10) : English Education

Sample Resume (1) : Publishing Company

Mijin Choi

45 Gaenari APT, Sanbon-dong, Suweon,

Gyounggi-do, Korea, 435-768

Phone (031) 398-2324

Email loveme77@yahoo.com

Career Objective :

Seeking a position to add developed expertise in a publishing company

Qualifications :

- 2 years publishing experience
- Fully bilingual in Korean & English
- Wide computer experience: Computer graphics, Program design
- Advanced writing skills

Educational Details :

Pacific University, Gyounggi-do, Korea

Bachelor of Arts in English, 2015

College Interests :

Editor of college magazine (1990 to 1994)

Career Experience :

City library Assistant (2012-2014)

Sales Clerk (Fall 2014-2015)

Writing Practice

Write your own resume to apply for a company.

(Positions : Publishing company or other related fields)

Sample Resume (2) : Accountant

Sangmi Lee
1234-2345 Misong Apt, Jung-dong
Anyang, Gyounggi-do, Korea, 113-432
Home No : 031-456-7645
Cell No : 010-2323-5432
Email : salang33@yahoo.com

Education Details :

Bachelor of Science (Accounting), February 2013
Sandra City University, Seoul, Korea

Work Experience :

Portfolio Accountant (Mary 2015 to Present)
Marketing Intern, E-Mart, Seoul (December 2013- May 2014)
Marketing Assistant, Lotte Mart, Busan (December 2012)

Expertise :

MS Word, Computer management program

Writing Practice

Write your own resume to apply for a company.

(Positions : Accountant company or other related fields)

Sample Resume (3) : Tourism and Hotel Management

David Park

567 Baker Street, Gangnam, Seoul, 221-344

Phone (02) 512 2367

Email davidpark@naver.com

ACADEMICS

Kookje University, Pyeongtaek, Korea

B.A. in Tourism Management, 2015

PROFESSIONAL EXPERIENCE

Byebye Tourist Agency, Seoul

Internship (November 2016- present)

- Management of tourist schedule and hotel management
- Assisted customers

Nightingale Airlines, Honolulu, Hawaii, USA

Internship (January 2015- May 2016)

- Worked on all aspects of the administration
- Activities of customers service

LANGUAGES KNOWN

Working knowledge of Chinese

Fluent in English

Writing Practice

Write your own resume to apply for a company.

(Positions : Tourism management company or other related fields)

Sample Resume (4) : Technical Writing and Editing

Jimmy Shim

9867 Maple Street, San Diego, CA, 234567

Home No : (567) 888-4590

Cell phone No : (019) 2323-0908

Email Id : Jimmy217@gmail.com

Objective :

A position of my experience and skills in technical writing and edit

Education Details :

Master of Science (Biological Sciences), Anticipated February 2016

University of New South Wales, Sydney, Australia

Bachelor of Science ((Biological Sciences), 2014

San Diego University, CA, USA

Writing Experiences :

Student Affairs, San Diego University (05, 2014 to present)

Writer and editor for Science and the World (Monthly student magazine)

Activities :

Lab Assistant (03, 2010 to 12, 2011)

Arranged and placed equipments in lab.

Computer Expertise :

MS Word, Excel, Pro Basic, Photoshop

Writing Practice

Write your own resume to apply for a company.
(Positions : Journalism or other related fields)

Sample Resume (5) : Business Administration

Jooyun Sung

213 Onions St. Sungnam, Gyeongigi-do, 987-543

Phone : (931) 219-6348

Email : jooyun345@google.com

EDUCATIONAL QUALIFICATION

Bachelor's Degree in Business Administration, Iowa University, Iowa, 2014

Seoul High School, Seoul, 2011

PROFESSIONAL EXPERIENCE

2016 - Present

Senior Information Representative

Trained computer system program.

2014 - 2015

Information Consultant, Safety Insurance Company

Helped the supervising team in PR department.

AWARDS & ACHIEVEMENTS

Best Business Administration, Iowa University, 2013.

Member of American Business Association.

CAREER HIGHLIGHTS

Received the Public Self-service Award in 2012.

Writing Practice

Write your own resume to apply for a company.

(Positions : Business Administration or other related fields)

Sample Resume (6) : Tourism Business

Haesong Kang
555 Southern Street, Opo, Gyeonggi-do 123-768
Phone : (522) 768-66775
E-mail : gangaji33@yahoo.com

Career Objective :

Seeking for a position in tourism business.

Qualification SumMary :

- Public social welfare license
- Well-traveled
- Intermediate-level Chinese
- Computer Expertise - MS Word, Excel, Photoshop

Education details :

Queen University, Ottawa, Canada
B.A. in Social Welfare, 02/ 2013

Career Highlights :

Children Center Tutor (2/ 2014 - Present)
Trained the children for elements of grammar and speech parts

Writing Practice

Write your own resume to apply for a company.
(Positions : Internship in tourism business or other related fields)

Sample Resume (7) : Information Technology

Younghyun Kim

289 College Street, Buchon, Chungchong-namdo, 23432

Cell phone : 015-2323-8765

Email : kimyh21555@hanmail.net

CAREER OBJECTIVE

Looking for an opportunity in the information technology.

PROFESSIONAL SKILLS

- Programming languages: BASIC, COBOL
- Other: Data structures, Database techniques

WORK EXPERIENCE

2012 - 2014 Summer Holidays

NATURE DELICIOUS RESTAURANT, Seoul

- Work as a waiter attending customers
- Receiving the deliveries and distributing
- Maintaining records

EDUCATIONAL DETAILS

Bachelor of Science in Computer programming, Western University, Seoul

May, 2012

EXTRA CURRICULAR ACTIVITIES

Member of Association of Machine Computing Personnel

Taekwondo, football, rock climbing

Writing Practice

Write your own resume to apply for a company.

(Positions : Information technology or other related fields)

Sample Resume (8) : Hotel

Hwarang Kim
467 Woods Street, Seoul, 512234
(013) 323-8686
hwarang66@google.com

CAREER OBJECTIVE

Culinary position in the fields of hotel.

PROFESSIONAL SKILLS

- 4 years of experience in culinary field.
- Hold good academic background in culinary arts.

WORK HISTORY

Cook (2012-Present), TWO SEASONS HOTEL, Seoul

- Helped chefs in the preparation of meal.
- Making sauces, baking, roasting and fries meat.

Cook (2009-2012), THE HIGH PRICE HOTEL, Seoul

- Preparing meal for the restaurant.

Prep Cook (2008 Summer), THE SEAFOOD HOTEL

- Keeping the record of food deliveries.

EDUCATIONAL BACKGROUND

Bachelor of Arts in Culinary Arts, 2008

The Culinary Institute of Orange University, London, UK

Diploma in Culinary Arts, 2007

Culinary Arts, The Western Food College, Paris, France

Writing Practice

Write your own resume to apply for a company.
(Positions : Culinary, hotel or other related fields)

Sample Resume (9) : Financial Services

Soyoung Min
456 Main Ave, Chunchon, Gangwon-do, 234-098
(016) 5665-2121
youngmin@hanmail.net

Career Objective

To obtain a beginner's position in a financial service company.

Professional Skills

- Strong knowledge of all economical trends.
- Excellent communication skills of economic works.

Work Experience

Internship, 2015-2016 winter

CREDIT FINANCIAL INC., Seoul

- Studied financial programs.
- Helped in finding policy.

Educational Qualification

February 2015

Bachelor of Science in Economics, College of Coconut, Seoul

Computer Skills

MS Word, Excel, PowerPoint

Other Interests

wind surfing, sport trainer.

Writing Practice

Write your own resume to apply for a company.

(Positions : Financial services company or other related fields)

Sample Resume (10) : English Education

Hyesong Kim
123-1345 Coconut APT, 456 Candy Street, Seoul, 354556
Cell phone : (019) 1234 6786
Email : banana33@yahoo.com

EDUCATIONAL QUALIFICATION

Bachelor of Education, February 2015
English Education, University of New South Wales, Sydney, Australia
Gaenari High School, Seoul, February 2010
Gaenari Middle School, Seoul, February 2007
Doremi Elementary School, Seoul, February 2004

CREDITS

- Received National Education Service Award in 2014
- Received gold award at Summer Writing Camp, Sydney in 2008

WORK HISTORY

Alternate Teacher, Hillary Middle School, The Philippines
March 2015 - May 2016

- Served as an alternative teacher

Student Teaching Practicum, North High School, Seoul, Korea
January 2013 - May 2014

- Teaching English writing and speaking

OTHER WORK

- Helped students' writing and report
- Member of Student Volunteers Group

Writing Practice

Write your own resume to apply for a company.

(Positions : Teaching at secondary school or other related fields)

저자 소개

정은주(Eun Joo Jeong)

영문학 박사 (세종대학교대학원 영어영문학과, 영미문학 전공)
현) 국제대학교 호텔관광경영계열 부교수

고인숙(Inn Sook Koh)

영문학 박사 (성균관대학교대학원 영어영문학과, 영미문학 전공)
현) 국제대학교 IT계열 부교수

심재황(Jaehwang Shim)

영어학 박사 (중앙대학교대학원 영어영문학과, 영어학 전공)
중앙대, 국제대 강사, 가천대 교육대학원 외래교수

Based on NCS
Four Seasons English
Listening & Speaking, Reading & Writing

1판 1쇄 인쇄 – 2017년 1월 10일
1판 1쇄 발행 – 2017년 1월 16일

저 자 - 정은주 · 고인숙 · 심재황
발 행 인 - 강 철 원
발 행 처 - 양 성 원
주 소 - 경기도 파주시 월롱산로 71(야동동)
전 화 - 031-946-3861(代)
팩 스 - 031-946-3864
이 메 일 - tnwpub@naver.com
출판등록 - 2015년 8월 31일 제 2015-000211 호

ISBN 979-11-87118-84-8

정가 17,000원